WONDERS OF THE
MOSQUITO WORLD

Wonders of the Mosquito World

BY PHIL AULT

Illustrated with photographs and charts

WORLD'S WORK LTD
The Windmill Press
Kingswood   Tadworth
Surrey

To Dr. George B. Craig, Jr.,
in gratitude for his help and enthusiasm

Illustrations courtesy of: *The Century Magazine*, 33, 34, 35; L.E.A., 40; The Library of Congress, 38, 39; Mosquito Genetics Project, University of Notre Dame, 49, 50, 51, 53, 54, 55; *South Bend Tribune*, 60; United States Department of Agriculture Photo, 8, 9, 10, 16, 21, 29, 30, 32, 36, 42, 43, 44, 45, 47, 61; United States Department of Agriculture Photo by Robert Bjork, title page; United States Department of Health, Education and Welfare, Public Health Service, National Medical Audiovisual Center, 6, 12, 14, 15, 18, 19, 22, 23, 24, 25, 27, 28, 58, 59.

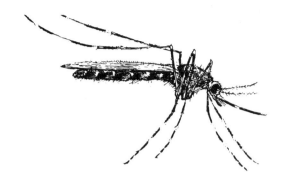

Contents

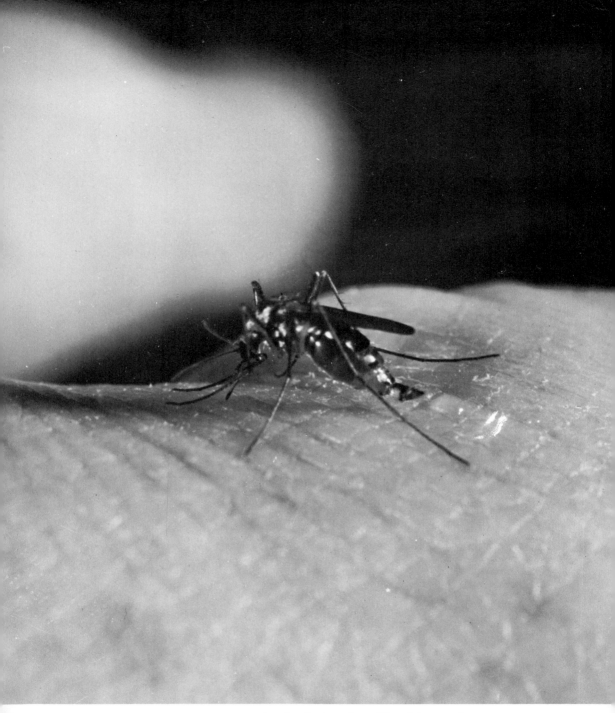

A familiar sight—a mosquito (Culicidae) sucking blood from a human arm

1

A Fascinating Villain

Many thousands of years ago, when the world was new and the people on it were happily free of trouble, legend tells of a mysterious locked box and a young girl named Pandora who had an overwhelming curiosity. One day when her curiosity grew too strong for the warnings she had received, she unfastened the magic cord tying shut the box.

As she opened the lid, out buzzed a swarm of angry insects. Immediately they attacked her. These were the troubles of the world—plagues and pestilence and grief—from which it would never be free again.

Pandora's Box and its escaped insects never existed except in legend. But we do know that mosquitoes are among the most ancient and bothersome insects in the world. They existed on earth before men did. Fossil remains of mosquitoes have been found in rocks on the Isle of Wight in the English Channel dating from the early Tertiary period of geological history about fifty million years ago. When we see a mosquito hovering over one of our bare arms, ready to land on the skin and suck in a meal of our blood, we slap at it in exactly the way our ancestors who lived in caves tried to kill the pests uncounted centuries ago.

The mosquito is sneaky. It hums around the room, keeping its intended victim awake and uneasy. He waits with a flyswatter, but the pest won't alight anywhere solid. Then when the victim relaxes for a moment it lands so gently on his arm that he doesn't feel it. The mosquito drinks its fill of blood. The victim slaps,

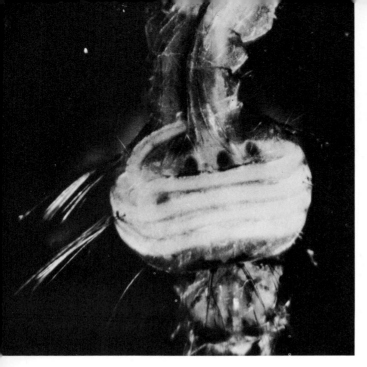

A mosquito larva fatally infected with a nematode (roundworm) which is coiled around the insect's thorax. The larva will not survive.

usually just too late. The mosquito drones contentedly away, leaving behind its calling card, an itching, stinging bump on the skin.

No matter how much we swat when outdoors on a moist, warm summer day, more mosquitoes arrive to plague us. Picnics and ball games and overnight camps are among their favorite places. Even when we sleep under netting and spray ourselves with mosquito repellant, they have a way of penetrating our defense.

If only Pandora had kept that girlish curiosity of hers under control!

Someone once asked, "Is there anything good about a mosquito?" The answer is no. It is an unloved and unwanted parasite; yet it thrives. The mosquito has no friends among men, and its only friends in the animal world are the tiny worms and protozoa that live in its body. No other creatures hurry to its assistance, although some are quick to devour it when the opportunity arises. Many animals are bothered by it as much as humans are, because it also bites them and makes them itch. The balance of nature seems to gain little from the existence of the mosquito, although a few fish, birds, bats, and insects eat mosquitoes as part of their diet.

All of man's effort to destroy it, including new scientific tools in recent years, have been inadequate, although important progress against it has been made in some areas. The stubborn mosquito remains among the most common of insects, turning up in all kinds of unexpected places. Its buzzing may be heard on mountains ten thousand feet high, or in damp coal mines four thousand feet underground.

These feather-light creatures look fragile, yet they have remarkable powers of survival. They can live in almost any kind of climate. Adapting themselves to different parts of the world, they have developed approximately 2,600 species, about 30 of them identified in the United Kingdom.

Cold or hot, moist or almost dry, no matter what the climate, the mosquito seems to be there. In the Far North, above the tree line on the shores of the Arctic Ocean, rugged species survive the cold. In northern Iceland, almost on the Arctic Circle, there is a lake named Myvatn, or "Mosquito Lake." Fishermen trying

Scientists placed mosquito larvae in these plastic boxes with screens at the bottom in a test area in Louisiana. Many varieties of parasites are being studied for their effectiveness in mosquito control.

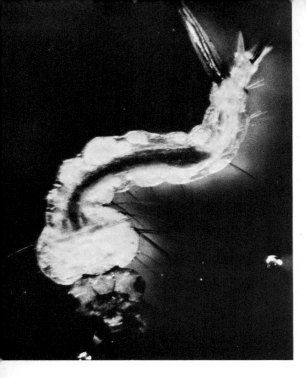

The white, swollen areas of infection in this mosquito larva indicate protozoan (a parasitic) disease.

their luck in the streams of northern Canada and Alaska during the brief summer report being attacked by mosquitoes "as big as horses." These Arctic mosquitoes are remarkably durable. Their larvae (the infant stage in the development of the insect) have been found frozen solid in the ice of ponds, yet after being thawed out have grown into hungry adults.

Even in hot desert oases, where only a few wells or a trickle of water exist to give the palm trees life, the familiar humming of the mosquito is heard.

At one time, apparently, a few remote Pacific islands were free of mosquitoes. Now they, too, are infested because modern travelers brought the insects with them without realizing that they were doing so. Probably the Hawaiian Islands were mosquito free before American whaling ships and missionaries arrived about 150 years ago. At least the moon seems safe from the threat of mosquitoes. Even if mosquitoes sneaked aboard a closely guarded spacecraft and landed on the moon, they couldn't survive because the moon's surface is without moisture.

Mosquitoes as well as Indians were waiting to greet the Pilgrims when they landed at Plymouth Rock in 1620. The colonists complained about the insects in letters back to England. In 1623 a pamphlet answering objections to Plymouth Colony was published in London. Written in the quaint English of the Pilgrims' day is this advice to others thinking about settling in the New World:

"They are too delicate and unfitte to begin new plantations and collonies that cannot enduer this biting of a mosquito."

Unfortunately we can't ignore mosquitoes, as we usually can ants, beetles, and earthworms, which go about their business without paying much attention to humans. Not the mosquitoes! They consider us their favorite targets. In some areas they are so thick that men avoid building their homes nearby.

For thousands of years men and women thought of mosquitoes only as nuisances to be avoided, hidden from, and slapped if possible. Even the wisest men of the royal courts had no idea that the mosquitoes are actual killers because they transmit deadly diseases.

Millions of people have been made sick, and often died, because mosquitoes had infected them with yellow fever, malaria, encephalitis, dengue fever, or filariasis.

These are diseases Americans don't hear much about now, because of the control work scientists have done. Malaria and yellow fever were dreaded by the early settlers in America, especially in the Southern states. The illnesses still afflict thousands of children and adults elsewhere in the world. One writer has stated that the malaria mosquito is "more dangerous than the crocodile, king cobra, or tiger."

Every year more people in the world are made sick by mosquito-borne diseases than by the illnesses we hear so much about, including cancer and heart disease. Most of the victims are in Asia and Africa. No wonder scientists are working so hard in their laboratories and in the field to eradicate the species!

Closeup of an Aedes *mosquito, female*

Luckily, the mosquitoes found around houses and play areas in North America, England, and Europe usually are the harmless varieties which do not carry disease. They are pests that irritate us and their itching bites are uncomfortable, but they are usually nothing to worry about.

The tropical portion of the earth is the most heavily infested with mosquitoes. Most disease-bearing species live in these regions, where temperatures and humidity are high and the heavy foliage in the rain forests near the Equator provides easy breeding places. The number of mosquitoes there is fantastic. Experiments have recorded nearly 30,000 mosquitoes in one acre. That would mean more than 16 million in a square mile!

Only within the lifetime of people still living, shortly before 1900, did brave scientific experiments prove that the mosquito in some forms actually is a villain. Although a villain, it is a fascinating one. When the scientists began studying it seriously, in efforts to save life, they found out more strange things about the mosquito than about most other insects.

2

Beware the Female

The mosquito and the common fly are related. Both belong to the biological order Diptera. Translated from Latin, this means "two wings," indicating that mosquitoes and flies have only one set of wings instead of the two sets common among flying insects. The word mosquito in Spanish means "little fly."

Scientists describe mosquitoes as the subfamily Culicinae, of the family Culicidae. The mosquito differs from many of its cousins in the fly family because it sucks blood, and because it has scales on its wings, body, head, and legs. The scales are much like those on a butterfly.

Actually, only the female mosquitoes suck blood—or bite, as we usually say. They are the troublemakers, carrying disease from one person to another by biting. Male mosquitoes are harmless, never attacking either humans or animals. If only male mosquitoes existed, nobody would be bothered by bites, and the world would not be plagued with mosquito-borne diseases.

Females bite to obtain a blood meal, which they must have in their bodies before they can lay eggs. In the mosquito world, females are the stronger sex. They live longer and fly farther. To produce body energy, they suck flowers, fruit, and the sugary fluids of plants. Males get their food from the same sources.

The male mosquito is attracted to the female by the humming sound she makes with her wings, beating scores of times a second. Two small hairy antennae project from the male's

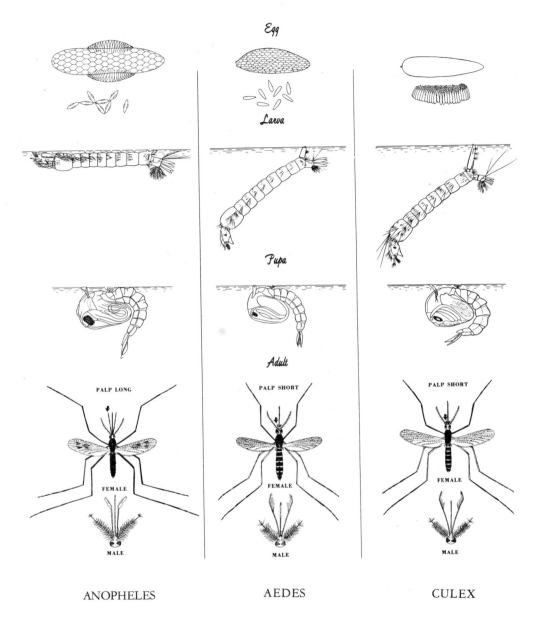

Egg

Larva

Pupa

Adult

PALP LONG   PALP SHORT   PALP SHORT

FEMALE   FEMALE   FEMALE

MALE   MALE   MALE

ANOPHELES   AEDES   CULEX

head, acting like ears. When they hear the female's hum they vibrate in unison, sending a message to the male's brain. Although nature makes many noises on a warm summer day, the

14

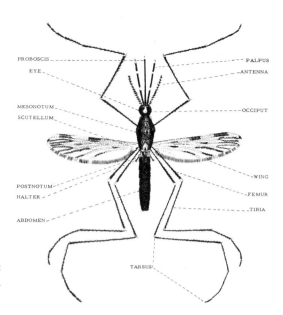

PROBOSCIS
EYE
MESONOTUM
SCUTELLUM
POSTNOTUM
HALTER
ABDOMEN
PALPUS
ANTENNA
OCCIPUT
WING
FEMUR
TIBIA
TARSUS

Body chart of an Anopheles *mosquito. Note long palps.*

male mosquito's sensitive hearing apparatus identifies the female's sound among them, and he flies to her for mating. The antennae of females have only a few tiny hairs, compared to the male's feathery ones.

Man-made objects sometimes mislead the male in his romantic quest, however. The hum of electric wires attracts him because it resembles the female's sound.

Similarly, a tuning fork at the right pitch when vibrated sounds so much like the female that it deceives the males. When a tuning fork is struck above a cage of males they become frantic, hurling themselves against the netting in an effort to reach the sound. Scientists in the field tried luring the males to their death with this artificial siren call, but the trick didn't work because the males were attracted from distances of only a few yards.

After the male emerges as an adult it is deaf for twenty-four hours, until its plume-like antennae dry and fluff out. During that time it cannot mate because it cannot hear the female's hum.

The head of a female mosquito (Southern house mosquito, Culex quinque-fasciatus). The eyes, short feelers (or palps), antennae, and proboscis are easy to distinguish. (See charts, pages 14 and 15)

Examined under a microscope, a mosquito's body is seen to have three sections—the head, thorax, and abdomen.

The Head—Projecting from the head are the organs with which the insect eats, sees, feels, and hears—the proboscis, eyes, feelers (or palpi), and antennae.

When the female lands on a person's arm, ready to bite, her weapon is a long, needle-shaped sucking tube, or proboscis. Since this is strong enough to pierce even the leathery skin of a frog or the overlapping scales of a snake, it makes easy work of penetrating the human skin.

The proboscis points forward from the mosquito's head between the pair of feelers that help her find her target. The bristle-like parts of this complicated little instrument are protected by a sheath called the labium. When the mosquito bites, the labium bends back, exposing the "business" parts of the proboscis. These include four slender scalpels that saw through the skin. A flexible tube in the proboscis pushes into the hole they make, and through this tube the female sucks up the victim's blood. Simultaneously she ejects saliva through another hair-like part of the proboscis into the wound, causing the itching in the bump raised on the human's skin.

The Thorax—This is behind the head, and is comparable to the human chest. The mosquito's six legs are attached to the thorax, the long rear pair stretching out behind the body. Also extending from the thorax are the mosquito's single pair of wings. These are veined and covered with scales. The arrangement of different-colored scales, forming spots, is one way some mosquito species are identified. Instead of a second set of wings, the mosquito has a pair of stubby knobs called halteres sticking out from the sides of the thorax. These function as gyroscopes, helping to control its flight by vibrating.

Humans and mosquitoes breathe in different ways. As a human draws in breath, the oxygen in the air passes through the lung membrane and into the blood stream, then circulates through the body. A man running hard grows short of breath and his muscles tire because he is burning up his oxygen supply faster than it reaches his muscle cells. A mosquito can drone on and on, beating its wings thousands of times a minute, without growing tired. It always has a large, quick supply of oxygen. In the mosquito, almost every cell is connected directly to the atmosphere by an individual breathing tube resembling a tiny straw. Respiratory gases are breathed out immediately through these tubes without circulating through the blood stream, as they do in humans.

The Abdomen—A mosquito sucks in a meal of blood heavier than her own normal weight. How can such a delicate, flimsy insect absorb all this burden? Nature has solved this problem by allowing the insect's abdomen to swell. The covering of the

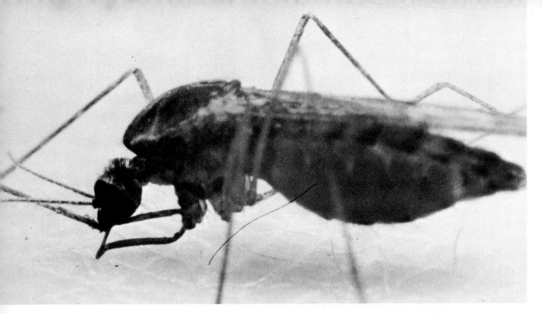

This photo of a female mosquito shows very clearly the hinged plates of the abdomen swollen with blood.

abdomen is not a shell, but a series of hinged plates held together by folded strips of almost transparent membrane. These membranes unfold as the blood is drawn in, permitting the abdomen to expand.

A mosquito that recently has absorbed a blood meal is easier to slap because she moves more slowly with her heavy load. During her first day as an adult, the female does not bite because a hormone from her brain must be turned on before she is ready to do so.

When a female carries a disease from one person to another, she is called a vector of that disease. First she bites a person ill with yellow fever, malaria, or one of the other diseases mosquitoes carry. She sucks the infected blood into her abdomen. As she flies around for the next few days, the infection continues to develop in her body. Her bodily processes break down the load of blood, and the disease organisms from it go into her salivary glands. Another element in the blood provides the protein needed by the eggs in her body, which she will deposit later. Hungry again, she bites another man, shooting the infection she carries into him through her saliva, much as a shot of serum is injected into a man's arm through the doctor's needle.

The physical differences among the 2,600 species of mosquitoes are tiny, but their living habits vary greatly.

In tropical forests especially, the various species live at different levels. Some stay close to the ground. Others live high up in the heavily leafed canopy of branches and vines. A man climbing a high tree can be bitten by one species, perhaps harmless, as he starts from the ground, and by a different, infectious kind when he reaches the upper limbs. In some forests natives escape being bitten at night by sleeping in tree houses, while to do this in other forests invites vicious attack.

For reasons scientists do not fully understand, some species never fly more than one hundred yards from their hatching place while others, seemingly with no more wing power, travel

The transmission cycle of arthropod-borne encephalitis, a disease that attacks the brain

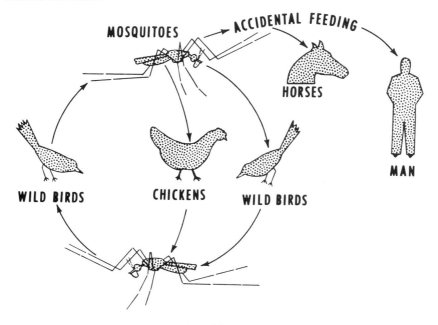

long distances. Flights of twenty miles are common, and flights of two hundred miles have been documented.

What attracts mosquitoes to humans, so they can find defenseless bare skin even in the dark? Why are some people bitten more than others, and why are some lucky ones rarely bitten at all?

Carbon dioxide in human breath is one attraction. This heavy colorless gas we exhale is like a "come hither" signal to the mosquito. A. W. A. Brown, a prominent researcher, demonstrated this by dressing two dummies like men and drenching them with carbon dioxide. The dummies were placed six feet apart. At first they did not attract certain species of mosquitoes. Then machinery inside the dummies exhaled carbon dioxide through their mouths at a normal breathing rate. Immediately the mosquitoes swarmed around their heads.

Notice how mosquitoes tend to buzz around your head more than the rest of your body. Caged mosquitoes will bite more readily after someone breathes on them.

Skin also gives off carbon dioxide, in less concentrated amounts. This, plus the warmth and moisture of the skin, draws the hungry insects. Warm-skinned individuals attract more mosquitoes than cool-skinned ones. In fact, experiments have shown that after a person's hand has been artificially cooled, it is less likely to be bitten. Odor plays a part in attracting mosquitoes, too. Blood, perspiration, and urine contain substances which attract mosquitoes.

The mosquito has a built-in heat detection system in its front legs, or tarsi, a kind of insect radar. When these detect heat waves from a body, the insect is drawn toward it.

This does not explain, however, why swarms of mosquitoes gather at times over fixed objects such as church steeples and chimneys. There are cases on record when the swarms have been thick enough to resemble smoke, causing people to sound fire alarms. Swarming usually occurs above or on the lee

20

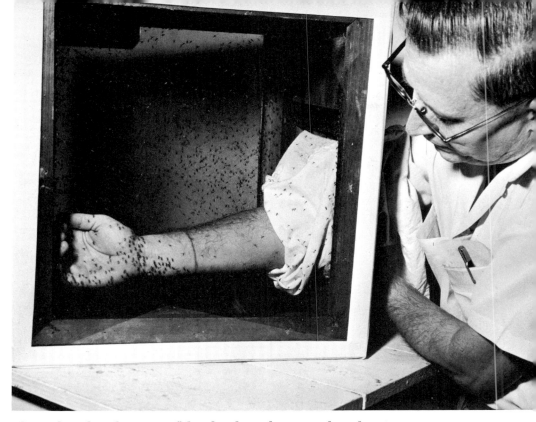

The carbon dioxide given off by the skin, plus warmth and moisture, attract hungry mosquitoes. The upper part of this scientist's arm has been treated with a repellant and the yellow-fever mosquitoes are avoiding it.

side of a prominent object. Hedges are favorite gathering places, too. Swarming has something to do with mating habits, and apparently is influenced by the intensity of light. Swarms of males fly back and forth in a sort of figure eight. Individual females fly into the swarm and mate.

Color and light influence the mosquito's habits, but how much is uncertain. Mosquitoes will land more frequently on dark clothing than on light. When animals are used as bait in experiments, mosquitoes are more likely to bite the darker-colored animals of a particular species than the lighter ones. In Africa, tests have shown that some mosquitoes will bite dark-skinned men more frequently than those with white skins.

3

How a Mosquito Grows

Once the male has found a mate, a fascinating process of life takes place. A few days after the female has taken a blood meal, she lays her eggs, usually between one hundred and three hundred of them, on water or at the water's edge. The eggs of some species are black, of others, light tan.

Strangely, while the adult mosquito is a land insect living in shrubbery, trees, or grass, the infant periods of its life are spent in water. Most mosquitoes deposit their eggs in still water—a pond or a puddle, rainwater in tree stumps, or moisture that has accumulated in man-made junk. A few species prefer running streams.

Many mosquito females lay their eggs in clusters, or rafts, about quarter of an inch in diameter, that float on the water.

LEFT: *Eggs of* Anopheles stephensi. RIGHT: *Eggs of* Aedes aegypti, *magnified forty times*

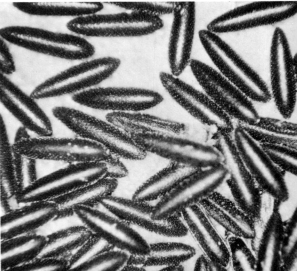

LEFT: Aedes triseriatus *larva*. CENTER: Anopheles stephensi *larva*. RIGHT: Culex quinquefasciatus *larva*

Others lay eggs singly on the water surface. These stay afloat because a sticky substance on their sides has air for keeping them buoyant. The *Aedes* species deposit their eggs just above the water's edge, so they will develop when the rising water dampens them.

Mosquito eggs hatch in one to three days and become larvae. However, the eggs of one important species, *Aedes aegypti*, can stay alive in dryness for several months; then when water touches the eggs, larvae emerge within minutes. This ability of *Aedes aegypti* eggs to survive in "dry storage" is one reason why this is a favorite type of mosquito for laboratory study. Eggs laid on paper under laboratory conditions can be sent from one part of the world to another by airmail.

The larvae live in water, usually just below the surface. Barely a millimeter long when they come from the egg, they grow to six or seven times that length in a week. In fact, the larval stage is the only time in its life that a mosquito grows.

In most species the larva hangs head down. Near its tail, attached to its abdomen, is a small siphon tube through which it obtains air. At the tip of the tube are five small lobes, like points of a star. These are closed when the larva is below water to prevent drowning. To breathe, the larva breaks the surface with its tube like a snorkel; the points open and it absorbs air. The open points cling to the surface film, holding the larva suspended.

The larva is growing, and it is hungry. Fortunately, it has machinery that enables it to eat while hanging upside down. Four sets of tiny hairy brushes near its mouth beat rapidly, stirring up currents of water from which bacteria of a suitable size are filtered. Also, the larva can close its breathing snorkel, drop below the surface, and feed on tiny plant life.

A lively wriggler, the larva moves jerkily about in the water by snapping the rear half of its body from side to side.

During the larval stage the mosquito is most vulnerable to its enemies. Water beetles, toads, dragonfly nymphs, and some shore birds like to eat the larvae. So do fish, particularly minnows. Despite these enemies, the number of larvae developing in summer is so enormous that mammoth swarms of mosquitoes appear almost simultaneously about ten days after a spell of wet weather has created new breeding places or caused rising water to make dormant eggs hatch.

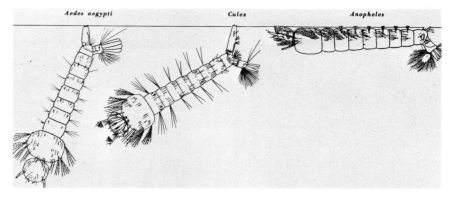

Drawing compares the breathing positions of larvae of the "big three" at the surface of the water.

Pupa of Aedes aegypti

As the larva grows it sheds its cuticle four times, each time revealing a new and slightly larger skin underneath. After about a week, giving a final jerk, it comes into a horizontal position just below the surface. A break appears in the cuticle of the thorax. Two breathing organs resembling tiny trumpets appear through the opening. These push through the water surface for air, the final larva cuticle falls away, and the developing mosquito has reached the third, or pupal, stage of its life.

The pupa looks like a comma, a round ball on top with the tail sticking down. Within the almost transparent pupal shell the adult body is forming. The pupa has been called the "dressing room" stage because of the changes that take place inside its shell. This lasts only two or three days. The pupa darts around the water by wriggling its abdomen, which ends in two paddles. It eats nothing, living on what the larva has devoured.

By making a series of somersaults, the pupa dives into deeper water. Having stopped these movements, it rises to the surface because it is lighter than water.

Suddenly the curled-up abdomen of the pupa straightens out along the surface, the back cracks open to form a launching pad, and out flies the full-grown adult mosquito. Its forefeet are covered with fine hair, so it can tread water as it launches itself. Quickly its wings harden in the air and carry it aloft. Its childhood is over.

25

4

The Big Three

Experts list three types of mosquitoes as the chief ones for men to worry about. Two of these are dangerous because they carry diseases. The third is the most common of the nuisance varieties. The "big three" are:

AEDES AEGYPTI

The yellow fever mosquito. Yellow fever causes severe headaches, high temperature, nausea, turns the victim's skin yellowish, and often is fatal. *Aedes aegypti* is the primary carrier of the yellow fever virus from one person to another, and is found mostly in the hotter parts of the world. In fact, the yellow fever virus will not develop in a mosquito when the temperature is below 68° Fahrenheit.

This mosquito likes to live near humans, whose carelessness in discarding junk helps this killer to spread. *Aedes aegypti* females frequently lay their eggs in artificial containers such as discarded cans and old tires that have caught rainwater.

In addition to yellow fever, *Aedes aegypti* transmits dengue, a tropical disease that causes acute illness and fever, also known as "breakbone fever"; encephalitis, which afflicts the central nervous system of men and animals, especially horses; and filariasis. This last disease produces fever, stiffness, and swelling. In severe cases the swelling becomes elephantitis, causing extreme enlargement of hands, feet, and other body parts.

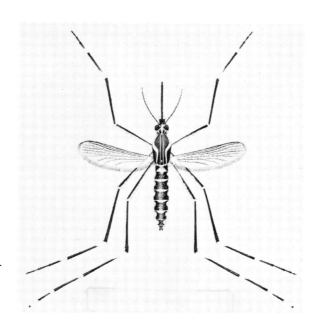

An adult Aedes aegypti *female*

Aedes aegypti has a unique trademark, a white design shaped like a lyre on the black back of its thorax. The joints of its legs are ringed with white, and there are white crossbands on the abdomen.

ANOPHELES

The malaria mosquito. There are about four hundred species of *Anopheles*, but only eighty-five are known to carry malaria. This ancient disease gives the victim headaches, fever, and severe chills, causes his spleen to swell, and leaves him weak. It can be fatal, unless properly treated.

The only way malaria can spread from one person to another is by the bite of the *Anopheles*.

Chinese mythology tells about the disease of three demons. One had a hammer, one a pail of water, and the third a stove, representing the headache, chills, and fever of malaria. Hippocrates, known as the "Father of Medicine," was familiar with

27

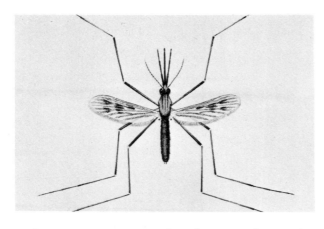

An adult Anopheles quadrimaculatus

malaria in B.C. 400. The disease always has been a curse of armies in hot countries. When a French general in Macedonia during World War I was ordered to attack, he replied that it was impossible because his army was in the hospital with malaria. Thousands of American and British soldiers suffered the same fate in Asia during World War II. Malaria has been the biggest disease problem in the Vietnam war, and some soldiers brought it home with them.

When *Anopheles* alights on a surface, the tail end of its body stands higher than its head, unlike the level posture of other mosquitoes. Four brown spots on each wing are a special marking of the malaria mosquito species found in the United States.

These two disease-bearing mosquitoes are such specialists in their deviltry that *Anopheles* can transmit malaria but not yellow fever, while *Aedes aegypti* has just the opposite capability. Yet both transmit filariasis.

CULEX PIPIENS

This pesky species is the common "house" mosquito found in the temperate parts of the world. Probably the mosquitoes buzzing around your neighborhood are *Culex pipiens*. Its close relative, *Culex pipiens fatigans*, lives in hotter areas and is dan-

28

gerous because it is the most important carrier of filariasis.

Culex pipiens breeds in standing water of any kind. It looks much like *Aedes aegypti* except for the latter's telltale markings. Why one species transmits disease and the other usually does not is a fascinating subject for study.

Among the lesser known mosquitoes are several with strange habits.

One, called *Wyeomyia*, lives nowhere but in the leaves of the pitcher plant, which oddly enough eats other insects. Another, the *Mansonia*, spends the early part of its life underwater, never coming to the surface until it emerges as an adult. This is possible because it has a snorkel-like breathing apparatus which it sticks into the underwater stems of plants. It draws its oxygen supply from the plant's fibers. The plant does the breathing for the *Mansonia* during its larval and pupal stages while man's

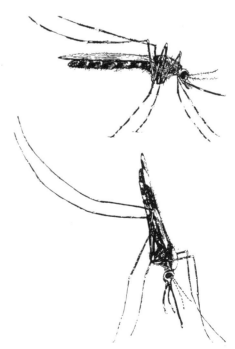

Culex *(top) and* Anopheles *compared in resting positions*

29

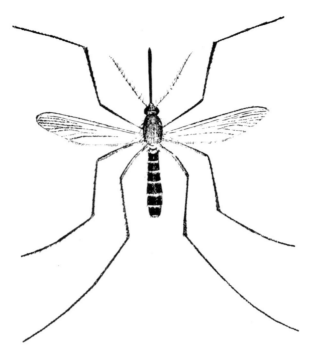

An adult Culex pipi-
ens *female*

efforts on the surface to eradicate the larva cannot reach it.

The mosquito with the strangest habit of all is the *Harpago-myia*, living in Asia and Africa. Instead of sucking blood or fruit for food, as most mosquitoes do, it robs ants.

This mosquito hovers over an ant's nest and awaits that industrious insect's return from a food-gathering expedition. As the ant tries to dodge, the mosquito stays directly in front of it until the ant is cornered. Thrusting its long proboscis forward, the highway robber mosquito puts the tip into the ant's mouth and sucks up a drop of regurgitated liquid.

Another puzzle of the mosquito world involves the time of day at which the various species bite. Of the "big three," *Aedes aegypti* is primarily a daytime biter while *Anopheles* usually attacks after dark. *Culex pipiens* bites most energetically at twilight, as anyone playing games in a field or walking along a stream at dusk can testify.

5

Detectives at Work

Medical detectives searching for the causes of deadly diseases have had adventures as exciting as, and sometimes more dangerous than, those of men who track down spies and criminals.

Among the greatest medical detective stories of history is the discovery that the *Aedes aegypti* mosquito causes yellow fever. Men had been dying in agony from yellow fever for many centuries. Nobody knew why, or how, to fight the disease.

Residents of the tropics dreaded the mysterious illness, which struck suddenly and seemingly at random. There were no clues as to why one man would catch yellow fever while others around him would not, when they lived under the same conditions, ate the same food, and worked side by side.

Then, in 1901, a group of investigators in Cuba led by Dr. Walter Reed, a United States Army officer, found the answer. They proved what a few men had suspected, but most had laughed at: yellow fever is carried from one man to another by a mosquito—not any mosquito but the one species, *Aedes aegypti.*

Today, yellow fever has been largely eliminated from many areas of the world. The doctor is remembered through the name of the Walter Reed Army Hospital in Washington, where Presidents and other famous men go for treatment. Almost forgotten, however, are the other men involved in the discovery, some of whom gave their lives to make it possible.

In the early days of the United States, "yellow jack"—as the

Whether a swamp is natural or man made, like this one, the still water is an invitation to mosquitoes.

fever was called—caused serious epidemics, especially in coastal cities like Philadelphia. When that city was the capital of the infant United States, a yellow fever epidemic in 1791 killed 10 per cent of the city's population. This evidence that Philadelphia was unhealthy was one reason why Congress decided to remove the national capital from there to the District of Columbia and build a new city to be named Washington.

The coastal epidemics were a puzzle. Why did yellow fever occur more frequently in seaports than in inland cities? Also, why did two or three weeks pass between the time one person became ill with yellow fever and the time anyone else in his family caught it?

The answers came as the result of the Spanish-American War, fought briefly in Cuba in 1898. Exciting clashes like the charge of Theodore Roosevelt's Rough Riders up San Juan Hill made the news in the war. Behind those headlines there was a grim fact. For every three American soldiers who died in battle, two died of yellow fever.

Soon the war ended, but the deaths from yellow fever did not. Many Americans remaining in Cuba after the Spanish surrendered were victims.

In Washington, Major Reed was appointed head of a team of investigators called the United States Army Yellow Fever Commission. His orders were, "Go to Cuba and find the cause of this disease."

Most doctors at that time believed that yellow fever was transmitted by soiled clothing and other articles that had become infected by a contact with the victim. A Cuban physician named Carlos Finlay had suggested in 1880 that yellow fever was transmitted by *Aedes aegypti*, and he did experiments with this species. Nobody believed him, however. His ideas were dismissed as ridiculous and almost forgotten.

Havana, the Cuban capital, was a hot, dirty city when the American medical team started work there. Another man who was to become famous in health work, Major William C. Gor-

Dr. Jesse W. Lazear (left) died of yellow fever in Cuba in 1900, during the first experimental work, as a result of a bite from a mosquito infected with yellow fever. John R. Kissinger (center) was a soldier who volunteered for the experiment and recovered from the fever. Dr. Walter Reed (right) headed the United States Army Yellow Fever Commission in Cuba. Note the mosquito design in the frame of these pictures.

Dr. Carlos Finlay was the first person to conduct experiments with the Aedes aegypti *mosquito. He concluded that it was this species of mosquito that conveyed yellow fever (1880).*

gas, took charge of cleaning up Havana. He did a splendid job, making the city a much more sanitary place. Other infectious diseases quickly diminished. Yellow fever did not; it continued to claim victims even in the cleanest part of the city. There had to be some other way the disease was transmitted than through filth. But what?

Hunting some new approach to the mystery, Reed remembered the experiments Dr. Finlay had conducted two decades earlier. He decided to pursue them, and see if the mosquito might indeed be the villain. He said, "We will have a mosquito bite a yellow fever victim, and then bite a man who is well. If the second man gets sick, the mosquito probably carried the disease to him."

Volunteers, mostly soldiers, were found to test this theory. Members of the Commission used themselves as human guinea pigs, too. A test tube containing a female mosquito was held against a sick man's arm while the mosquito sucked in a meal of blood. Later the test tube was pressed against a healthy man while the captive mosquito bit him.

At first nothing happened. Several kinds of mosquitoes were

tried. The doctors didn't know yet that to carry the disease a mosquito had to bite a sick man during the first three days of his illness. And it had to be an *Aedes aegypti*. Then Dr. James Carroll, a member of the Commission, became seriously ill after being bitten in a test. Fortunately, he recovered. The searchers were encouraged, but not absolutely sure. A soldier volunteer was bitten, became ill, and eventually recovered, just as Dr. Carroll had. Another Commission member, Dr. Jesse W. Lazear, was bitten on the back of his hand by an *Aedes aegypti*. He fell ill with yellow fever and died within a few days.

Clearly, the mosquito had carried the disease in each case.

Dr. Gorgas and his men took on the gigantic task of trying to eliminate *Aedes aegypti* from Havana. No such campaign against a single species of mosquito had ever been attempted. They made a house-to-house search for breeding places. The killer mosquitoes were found breeding in cisterns, jugs of water, even the holy water fonts of churches. A new law required that every container of water in Havana must either be covered or have kerosene spread on it. Kerosene kills mosquito larvae by forming a coating on the water surface through which their

Dr. James Carroll, the first man to become ill of yellow fever after being bitten by an Aedes aegypti *during the experiments conducted in Cuba by the Commission.*

35

breathing tubes cannot penetrate for oxygen.

Instead of helping Gorgas, many Cubans thought the inspection was silly and tried to trick the inspectors. Gorgas persisted, however.

The campaign succeeded, within six months. Havana had never been without a case of yellow fever for a single day since 1762. Now, for the first time in 140 years, the city was completely free of the disease.

Further study showed that seaport cities were the most frequent places for yellow fever outbreaks because *Aedes aegypti* liked being close to men, and often was carried from country to country aboard ships. In the days of sailing ships, the open casks of water on decks were a favorite breeding place. Yellow fever and the *Aedes aegypti* mosquito were introduced into the Western Hemisphere aboard ships in the slave trade during the 1600's. Both disease and insect originated in tropical Africa.

The delay in infecting other persons was explained, too. After a mosquito has bitten a sick person, it must carry the virus in its own body for one to three weeks while the germ develops. Only after this change occurs will the virus be infectious when shot into another person by the mosquito.

A few years after the victory of Reed and Gorgas in Havana, the United States made the decision to build the Panama Canal. The route for the fifty-mile waterway ran through the jungles of the Isthmus of Panama, from the Atlantic to the Pacific. The French had tried to build a canal there twice but they had been forced to give up, partly because of poor management but mostly because the French company's workers had been stricken so often with the disease.

Gorgas was promoted to colonel and went to Panama as chief sanitary officer of the project. Using the knowledge and stern methods developed in Cuba, he soon had yellow fever whipped

Female Aedes aegypti, *the yellow fever mosquito*

37

Dr. William Gorgas cleaned up Havana to free the city of yellow fever, and later went to Panama as chief sanitary officer on the canal project. He was photographed here as a major general.

in that area. Work moved ahead with a healthy crew of builders. When the first ship steamed through the Panama Canal in 1914, Gorgas was there to cheer it, and to be cheered. The world knew that he and others who had tracked down the *Aedes aegypti* deserved much credit for the day's triumph.

Only a few years earlier scientists had at last unlocked the mysteries of malaria.

Hippocrates observed more than two thousand years ago that this fever claimed most of its victims around swampy areas. They assumed that it was transmitted by the foul, moist swamp air. In fact, the name malaria literally means "bad air." Ancient medical men urged that the swamps be drained. When they were, the malaria diminished. They had taken the right step for the wrong reason. They did not realize that the disease was

38

carried from person to person by the mosquitoes that bred in swamps, not by the air itself.

Doctors began to suspect a connection between malaria and mosquitoes in the 1880's. Several of them worked on the problem separately in Italy, North Africa, England, and Asia.

The man who finally proved the connection was Dr. Ronald Ross, a British Army surgeon stationed in the remote hill country of India. He let *Culex* mosquitoes feed on malaria patients, then bite healthy men, but the disease was not transmitted. He put malarious mosquitoes in water to die and had men drink the water, but again nothing happened. This convinced him that malaria was not transmitted through water. Similar experiments with *Aedes aegypti* failed.

In 1897 Ross captured brown-spotted *Anopheles* females in the hills and tried them. This time he succeeded in transmitting malaria to test patients. He dissected a biter under a microscope

Work goes ahead in the Panama Canal cut at Culebra, 1904. The Canal was finished because of Gorgas, who controlled the mosquito that carried yellow fever.

and saw the malaria parasite developing in the mosquito's stomach wall.

Ross was awarded the Nobel Prize for his work in 1902 and, after being knighted by King Edward VII, became known to the world as Sir Ronald Ross.

Since the yellow fever and malaria mosquitoes were identified as killers many decades ago, and vigorous steps taken against them, perhaps you wonder why they still cause so much sickness. If men know so much, why haven't mosquito-borne diseases been wiped out almost completely, as poliomyelitis has been? The problem is much like enforcing the law. Detecting the criminals is only part of the job; arresting them is equally difficult.

Sir Ronald Ross who discovered that mosquitoes transmit malaria.

6

Men vs. Mosquitoes

The mosquito's natural enemies were attacking it long before men realized how dangerous it is. They didn't do a good enough job to reduce the mosquito population, however.

A bat can eat seven hundred mosquitoes an hour. Dragon-flies devour them, too. So do lizards, spiders, and some birds, especially house martins and swallows. But the mosquito population kept growing despite these enemies. As more men populated the earth, they carelessly created more artificial breeding places. Such tremendous numbers of larvae were astir in the water that the combined efforts of birds, fish, and other natural foes could kill off only a fraction of them.

As we have seen, the Greeks and Romans accidentally used the first man-made controls against mosquitoes by draining swamps to remove the supposedly poisonous swamp air. Hundreds of years later, right up to 1900, this was still the primary method used.

When scientists finally discovered that mosquitoes carried death, man's war against the insects began in earnest.

People protect themselves against adult mosquitoes by sleeping under netting and behind screens. We spray ourselves with insect repellents. These measures protect individuals, but do nothing to eradicate the pests. The big campaigns for that purpose are frequently aimed at their breeding places. Killing a thousand larvae is easier than killing a thousand adults.

A primitive form of control, used in native villages, is to put

A man applying oil to puddles in an attempt to prevent mosquitoes from breeding

minnows in pools where mosquitoes are known to breed. The minnows eat the larvae.

Several control methods use the principle that most larvae get air by pushing their breathing tubes up through the surface of the water. If they are prevented from doing so, they perish. Men spray stagnant pools with oil or kerosene, which form a film on the water that the tubes cannot penetrate. Detergent spread on water has the same effect. It reduces the surface tension so the larvae cannot cling to the surface and therefore sink.

Unfortunately, these methods do only part of the job. Oil sprays do not work well on the moving water of streams, where some mosquitoes breed. They cannot be used on ponds or reservoirs from which humans and animals take water. Reaching all casual water with sprays is almost impossible, no matter how hard men try, because mosquitoes deposit their eggs in the water in cavities as small as the hoofprints of a horse on a dirt road.

Although most species breed in fresh water, some have

42

adapted to salt water, making the control problem on marshy coasts even more difficult. The salt marshes along the New Jersey shore are notorious for their mosquitoes. Recent outbreaks of mosquito-borne encephalitis have occurred in this area, causing death to both humans and horses.

Scientists in California have discovered that the sticky seeds of mustard plants and certain other weeds can be used against larvae. When dropped into water, these seeds produce a coating of mucilage. The larvae are trapped when their mouth brushes stick in the gluey substance as they beat the water for food. The experimenters heated the seeds to 250° Fahrenheit to sterilize them so they wouldn't spread weeds. If field tests are satisfactory, large quantities of mustard plant seed can be grown for this purpose.

In the years before World War II, public health experts turned to the chemists for better methods than oil spraying and drainage.

These scientists tried a compound called Paris green, a poisonous copper-arsenic dust. This proved to be superior to oil as a spray because it could be used on slowly moving water and could be sprayed by hand, blower, or airplane. Also, it did not harm fish or animals. Soon tons of Paris green were being sprayed on waters in many countries. This process had to be repeated weekly, a tedious and expensive task.

In 1943, DDT preparations that proved effective as aerosols in laboratory tests were tried out of doors against mosquitoes in cages.

During World War II, much mosquito research was conducted because of the jungle warfare. Here soldiers test a mosquito repellant face cream in 1942.

During World War II, when thousands of soldiers in the Pacific war zone were being stricken with malaria, fresh efforts were made to develop an even better chemical weapon against mosquitoes. The product that emerged from this search was spectacular in its power and soon became a household word—DDT.

Actually, DDT wasn't a new compound. Away back in 1874 a German pharmacist named Othmar Ziedler synthesized alcohol, chlorine, and sulphuric acid into dichloro-diphenyl-trichloroethane. Little use was made of the discovery. Few people could pronounce it and nobody realized its values as an insect killer.

Many years later a Swiss company, hunting a new method for mothproofing, experimented with it. Paul Müller, a company chemist, tried the compound on flies and found that in either spray or dust form it killed huge numbers of them. He found, too, that the effectiveness of the chemical lasted a long time, far longer than other sprays such as Paris green. Müller received the Nobel prize in medicine for his discovery.

The British shortened the many-syllabled word to simple DDT. Manufacture of DDT began in the United States and Great Britain during World War II, and before the conflict ended it was destroying disease-bearing insects in such spec-

44

tacular numbers that public health officials were amazed at their good fortune.

DDT does not kill insects instantly. They show no outward reaction immediately after contact with it, but a few minutes later fall into a paralyzed spin and die.

Months after a surface has been treated with DDT, insects touching it are killed. This lasting power was important, because once an area had been sprayed it did not need a follow-up visit for many weeks, and the control teams could move on to other disease-ridden communities.

The marshes of the Tiber River delta near Rome, infested with malaria since ancient times, were used for a major test of DDT.

All buildings in the port of Ostia and other delta towns were

This tide gate is closed by the pressure of the high tide, thus preventing flooding of salt marsh in Florida. Conversely, pressure of rain water in the diked land opens the gate, permitting marsh to drain and thus reducing mosquito breeding sites.

sprayed with it. No other control measures were used, to give it a true test. Almost immediately the malaria rate dropped. A report on the experiment said, "Not one new case of malaria was found in the Tiber Delta, and Ostia achieved a state of health she had not enjoyed in 2,000 years."

At last men seemed to have found the means to control the mosquito. The Rockefeller Foundation, the World Health Organization, and governments around the world spent millions of dollars in spraying disease-laden areas with DDT. The cost was too great to use the chemical on a large scale in areas where only nuisance mosquitoes lived. The work must be done in countries afflicted with malaria, yellow fever, dengue, and filariasis.

In India, for example, amazing success was achieved. Before 1952, when the campaign began, seventy-five million Indians a year suffered from malaria. One victim in each ten died. By 1965, the spraying was so sucessful that the annual number of cases had dropped to 100,000!

Then two disturbing facts developed. The stubborn mosquitoes were fighting back. Their bodies adapted themselves to the new enemy, and they developed immunity to DDT. Spraying no longer killed every mosquito that made contact with the chemical. The malaria rate in India rose again, nowhere near the level of the old days, but substantially.

In the southern United States, the government spent $53 million during the 1960's trying to wipe out the *Aedes aegypti* mosquitoes. Not a single case of yellow fever had been reported in the United States for forty years, and *Aedes aegypti* is harmless unless it has an infected person to bite. Nevertheless, there was fear that potentially dangerous mosquitoes might migrate on ships and airplanes from Central and South America, where the disease exists.

DDT spraying and other methods were used for five years, but the mosquitoes hung on. Finally the government gave up, stating that hundreds of millions of dollars would be needed,

Agricultural Research Service entomologists are looking for better ways to use present insecticides while testing new ones. This fine mist is being sprayed from ultra-low-volume apparatus.

and even then success would be uncertain.

The mosquito was far from defeated.

Equally alarming was the second unexpected development. Evidence appeared that the same long-lasting effect which made DDT so valuable against mosquitoes was killing fish, birds, and game. The deadly chemical, turned loose in large amounts, was upsetting the delicate balance of nature.

Leaders in the conservation movement were alarmed by finding heavy amounts of DDT in fish and animals. They demanded that the use of DDT be stopped, arguing that the good it did was outweighed by the long-range harm it caused. Now its use is strictly controlled by law in many countries.

Once again it was up to the scientists. They must seek additional, and safe, ways to destroy the infectious mosquitoes.

47

7

Mosquitoes Made to Order

A radically new way to wipe out mosquitoes became the goal of researchers. They turned to the science of genetics, to manipulate the lives of mosquitoes by scientific breeding. Gradually a question formed in their minds: "Can we make the mosquito population commit suicide?"

The idea sounds fantastic, but biologists think it may work. Already in the laboratories they have developed strains of mosquitoes that can breed themselves completely out of existence. Instead of killing off the dangerous insects by sprays and other physical controls, the scientists seek to reduce the population by limiting the number of mosquitoes born. This is known as genetic control.

Genes are the elements in a body which transmit characteristics from one generation to the next. Every characteristic of an individual that can be inherited is passed along from parent to offspring through the genes in the reproductive cells. An individual receives a set of genes from each of its parents.

When individual mosquitoes having certain characteristics mate with those having other characteristics, their offspring are different from either parent. By adding new characteristics in succeeding generations, biologists eventually can "manufacture" a strain of mosquitoes quite unlike its ancestors in certain aspects.

Researchers using this method in their laboratories have produced weird new kinds of mosquitoes, unlike any that nature

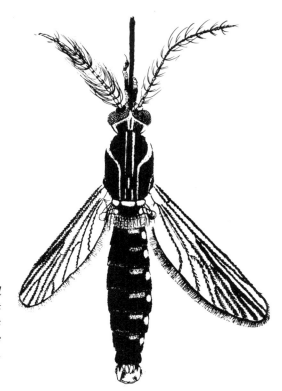

This laboratory-created mosquito is male on its left side and female on its right side. Notice the differences in antennae and structure.

has created. These "remodeled" mosquitoes with their distinctive markings are opening fields of knowledge that may eventually save the lives of men, women, and children who might become victims of disease-carrying mosquitoes.

Much of the genetic experimenting is done with the yellow fever mosquito. The genetic lessons learned from *Aedes aegypti* will be applied to other species. The short life span of the adult mosquito helps the research. Within a few weeks, geneticists can watch the bodily changes develop through several generations.

World headquarters for producing "custom made" yellow fever mosquitoes is the Mosquito Genetics Project at the University of Notre Dame at South Bend, Indiana in the U.S.A. In its laboratories, as moist and warm as a flower hothouse, ten

Two Aedes aegypti *larvae. The one on the left is normal; on the right is a mutant yellow larva. This is the first mutant found in* Aedes aegypti.

million mosquitoes are kept. Some fly around rooms with heavy netting at the doors. Others are held captive in hundreds of round cardboard ice cream containers covered with tight net, each container carefully labeled. Thousands of larvae and pupae wiggle in white enameled pans.

Laboratory workers in white coats keep charts of all the breeding combinations used, so they know exactly how they obtain each new strain, or mutant. Once a desired mutant has been developed, it can be mass produced like a factory product.

The scientists need to know everything possible about the living habits of the dangerous species, in order to control them. How far will they fly? Which of the 2,600 species will mate with each other? How do they react to heat and light? How do they change their bodies to meet new conditions?

The best way to get answers is to watch the individual insects under natural living conditions. One big difficulty comes in trying to identify the individuals because all the mosquitoes in a swampy field, for example, look so much alike. The Notre Dame biologists are solving the problem by developing strains with odd physical characteristics called genetic markers. These can be identified easily when field workers collect a mass of specimens.

One mosquito created in the laboratory has feet growing from its nose. Specimens have been created with eyes of seven different colors.

Among the strangest custom-made mosquitoes are those with two sexes. The front half of one mutant is female and the rear half is male. Behavior of a mosquito is mainly controlled by the sex of its head. Since the female instinct is to feed on blood, this she-he mosquito does so and often dies, because its midsection is male and cannot absorb blood. So it ruptures. The male rear

This mosquito created at the University of Notre Dame has both male and female antennae, plus eyes of two different colors.

4

section can mate with a normal female and produce normal off-spring.

There is a reverse double-sexed model, too, with the front half male and the rear part female. This he-she mosquito is unable to reproduce itself. There is even a third variation: the left side male with its bushy antenna, and the right side female. These sex changes are brought about when two sperm, one female-determining and one male-determining, fertilize a single egg.

Control of time and temperature is vital in scientific breeding. For some purposes the mosquito must be "processed" within an hour after it emerges from the pupal stage into adulthood. This need has led to creation of an ingenious mosquito harvesting machine in the laboratory. Its use removes the need to keep a minute-to-minute watch over the birth of adult mosquitoes. A large revolving plastic disc contains a hole. Petri dishes of water containing pupae are placed in a circle, one for each hour. Every hour a clock mechanism advances the disc one hole, and the mosquitoes born during that hour are released upward into a marked container.

Another machine helps the laboratory men determine which strains of the insects are most active physically, and thus able to range farther afield carrying disease.

This device records the movements of a single mosquito for twenty-four hours. A plate lined with copper strips carrying alternate positive and negative electric charges is placed under a glass container. Inside, a mosquito is kept in darkness. Each time the mosquito touches down on the plate, its feet complete an electrical circuit and a tiny mark is made on a recording tape. This shows the amount of the insect's activity. But there are mysteries remaining. Experiments may prove that a certain species is most active at 3:00 A.M., but we still do not know why this is so.

Manipulation of the mosquitoes' sex holds intriguing possi-

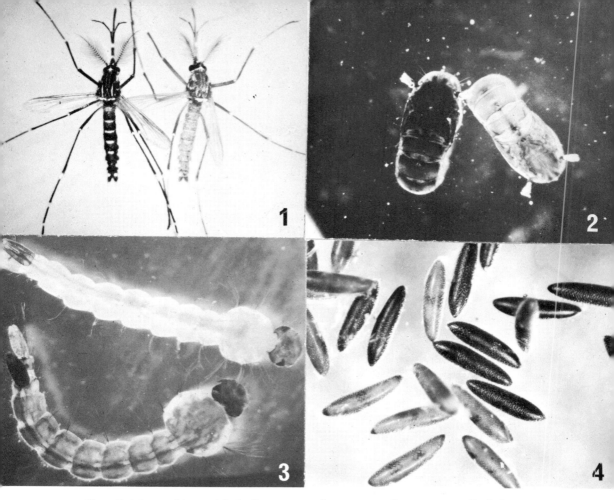

Geneticists working with Aedes aegypti *have created a mutant called the Bronze. Photo 1 shows an adult normal male on left, the Bronze mutant on right; Photo 2 shows the normal pupa on left, the Bronze pupa on right; Photo 3 shows the normal larva below and the Bronze on top; Photo 4 shows a mixture of normal and Bronze eggs.*

bilities in controlling the population. The fewer females there are, the fewer new mosquitoes will be born. One strain has been developed at Notre Dame in which 95 per cent of the newborn mosquitoes are males. This lopsided ratio is carried on to each new generation, every twelve days, until the females have disappeared and the mosquito strain dies out. In a laboratory experiment, a test population of this strain bred itself completely

Mosquito larvae are kept in enameled pans, carefully classified. Dr. George B. Craig, Jr., director of the Mosquito Genetics Project (left), and Dr. William Hickey watch a laboratory worker put a pan of developing insects into a rack.

out of existence in forty-two weeks.

Geneticists have created a mutant called the Bronze which has become extremely valuable as a genetic marker.

The eggs and bodies of *Aedes aegypti* are black because of the presence of a compound called melanin. In the Bronze, scientists have been able to prevent the formation of melanin. As a result, the eggs and the adults are light tan or bronze, making them quickly identifiable in a mass of ordinary mosquitoes. Also, the absence of melanin makes the eggs defective. They usually die within twelve hours after being laid. Without fertile eggs to produce larvae, the strain eventually dies.

Still another laboratory device is really a trick against the female mosquitoes. Researchers led by Dr. George B. Craig, Jr., director of the Notre Dame laboratory, tested many strains and found that the female in each test group is monogamous. This means that she will accept only one mate.

The scientists then developed a hormone called Matrone. When a female mosquito is sprayed with this hormone she is fooled into thinking that she has accepted a mate, and the process by which she lays eggs is halted. Thus she is eliminated as a possible mother of a new mosquito generation.

Of course the big question is how well these ingenious methods developed in the laboratories will work in the field. Discoveries that seem of great value in the laboratory sometimes fail when tried under natural conditions. There may be difficulty in reaching enough suitable mosquito masses, the weather may play tricks, or other unpredictable factors in nature may arise. Thus long testing under arduous field conditions is needed before specific genetic control methods are put into mass use.

During one recent spring more than 100,000 male mosquitoes with genetic markers were released in field tests in Mississippi by the United States Public Health Service. Many of them were recaptured and the pattern of their activities analyzed.

The World Health Organization has been making tests of the new methods in Asia and Africa. A recent test in a Burmese village overrun with infectious mosquitoes shows what can be achieved. Geneticists found by experiments that a type of mosquito common in Fresno, California, was incompatible with a Burmese strain that transmits filariasis. That is, a mating of the

Actual mosquitoes used in the Mississippi field tests. The mosquito on left is normal adult male, the one on right carries a silver genetic marker, the one in the center is a mixture of the two strains, which resulted from breeding in the field.

two strains would not produce any offspring.

A German scientist took a mass of the California mosquitoes to the village of Okpo. Each day he set free five thousand of the sturdy American males. They numerically overwhelmed the males of the Burmese species and soon mated with the Okpo females. The females started laying infertile eggs. Since the eggs would not hatch, the number of mosquitoes in Okpo began to dwindle after the current crop had lived out its life cycle. After two months, Okpo was free of mosquitoes.

Results of this sort excite scientists. They see them as pointing to the day when man can overcome the mosquito population without harming the birds and animals we cherish and need. The most practical method appears to be reduction of the mosquito population by larval control and chemical spraying, then use of genetic control to wipe out the stubborn survivors.

Even so, the problem of mosquito control is so massive that nobody is foolhardy enough to predict the day when any species of mosquito is banished from the earth.

More knowledge must be acquired in the laboratory. Huge amounts of money and labor must be used in applying this knowledge in the field. This will be done almost entirely in those areas of the world, especially in Asia and Africa, where the disease carriers thrive.

Only after the infectious species are defeated will governments and scientists be able to conduct a full-scale campaign against nuisance mosquitoes, using all the weapons science has developed. Efforts to keep down the number of pests by spraying and drainage will continue around well-populated areas, but these are not enough. Away from the cities the mosquitoes are still largely unchallenged, except by their natural enemies. So prepare to keep swatting. At least it is encouraging to know that science appears to be started along the right track toward freeing men from this insect plague that has been afflicting the world for thousands of years.

8

For Mosquito Watchers

When handled with care, so they don't get loose and upset other members of the family, mosquitoes are fun to study. They don't need much space, and the equipment can be simple. But be careful. If your laboratory specimens escape and buzz around the house, your parents may quickly lose enthusiasm for your project.

The most interesting way is to obtain mosquito eggs and watch the entire life process. With some searching in the right places in spring, you probably can find rafts of eggs. Stagnant pools, especially in areas of woods or heavy foliage, are among the best places to look. A good time is two or three days after a heavy rain. The rafts of eggs can be scooped up and carried home in small containers of water. In most parts of the temperate zone, the eggs found by searchers will be those of the nuisance *Culex pipiens.*

Rafts of *Culex* eggs can be purchased from biological supply houses if your hunting luck isn't good.

After the eggs have hatched, pour the larvae into a container. Round cardboard ice cream cartons are good for this purpose. Pint-sized ones often are used in laboratories. Fill one halfway with tap water, and put no more than fifty larvae into it. Overcrowding will slow their growth.

About ten to fourteen days pass while the eggs develop into larvae, then pupae, and finally adults.

With a magnifying glass or microscope, you can watch the

Rafts of Culex *eggs can be scooped out of water or purchased from biological supply houses.*

Drawing shows the life cycle of an Anopheles *mosquito.*

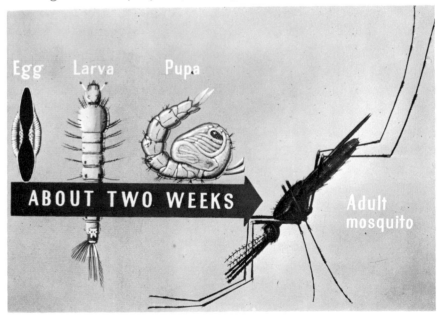

Egg   Larva   Pupa

ABOUT TWO WEEKS

Adult mosquito

A warning of what can happen if containers of water are left standing uncovered

larvae wriggle from the egg cases as they hatch. Larvae must have food. Small pellets of dog food dropped into the water every day or so provide this. They stimulate bacterial growth on which the larvae feed. Bread crumbs will work, too.

Keep your experimental area warm, around 80° Fahrenheit if possible, and at high humidity, for best growing conditions. At cooler room temperatures development will be slower. The amount of light is unimportant.

By watching your specimens closely, you can see the larvae turn to pupae after five or six days. The pupal stage is the time when the adult body develops. This change is visible through the cuticle. Finally comes the fascinating moment when the adult mosquito emerges from the pupal shell, dries its wings,

59

and takes off from its launching pad in the water. Don't forget to make certain that it flies into a container, not into the open air!

Remove the lid and bottom from a second ice cream container and turn it upside down. Cover the upper opening with gauze drawn tight, then place this container on top of the first one. As the mosquitoes hatch they will rise up into the top container. Quickly replace the lid, and you have a container of mosquitoes to watch. A slice of apple placed on the gauze cover will provide food for your specimens.

Adult mosquitoes can be caught by putting out slices of apple or solutions of sugar water. When the mosquito alights to feed, it can be trapped with an ice cream container or a test tube. Place some moist cotton in the bottom of a test tube. Catch a mosquito engorged with blood in the tube and plug the end

A "junk yard" like this helps to increase the mosquito population. Such areas should be cleaned up.

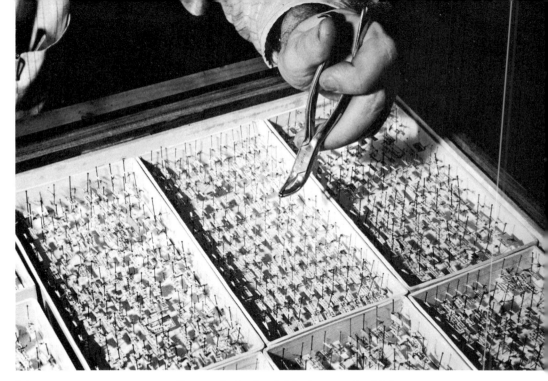

Mosquito specimens are vital to study in the field of mosquito biology.

with dry cotton. If she is an *Aedes* she will deposit her eggs in the cotton. After four or five days, the eggs will be developed and ready to hatch. Just fill the tube with water and let it sit a day or two.

If you don't mind becoming a "blood brother" with a mosquito, let one land on your arm to bite, then trap it instead of squashing it. The best time of day for catching mosquitoes is at dusk, when they are most active.

With a magnifying glass you can determine whether your captive is a male or female by the amount of plumage on its antennae. Other parts of the body can be studied, too.

Students of mosquitoes can learn about control methods, while doing their families a favor, by inspecting their homes to remove breeding places for the insects. Check to see that no buckets containing water are left around the yard, and that old tires have not been discarded where they can accumulate water.

Point out to your parents or other adults the potential breeding places in junk cars, empty oil drums, and other debris on the property. Also, show them puddles of standing water that fail to drain off after heavy rains. If these breeding places on your property are eliminated, the number of mosquitoes around your home should diminish.

The field of mosquito biology is just developing. Exciting discoveries about these obnoxious and sometimes dangerous pests will be made in the next few years. Many of the men and women scientists who will make them will start their studies as boys and girls with simple observations at home. Perhaps you will be among them.

Index